Manta Ray

By: Beth Costanzo

There are so *many creatures* in our seas and oceans. Some of them are extremely large (like *orca whales*) and some of them are extremely small (like *plankton*). Some *sea creatures* need to keep moving to breathe while others can stay still and be just fine.

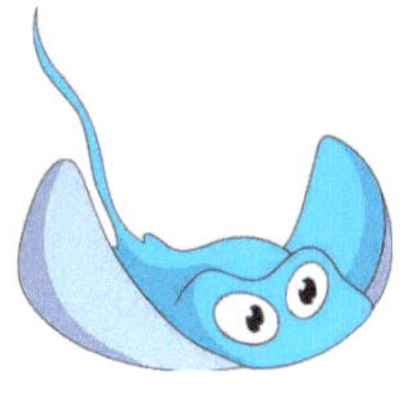

Today, we want to take a deeper look at one of the most fascinating creatures swimming around in our seas. It is the **manta ray**. The **manta ray** is fascinating for so many reasons. Whether you are just hearing about the **manta ray** or have actually seen a real one at your local aquarium, let's explore what makes manta rays so cool.

An Introduction to the Manta Ray

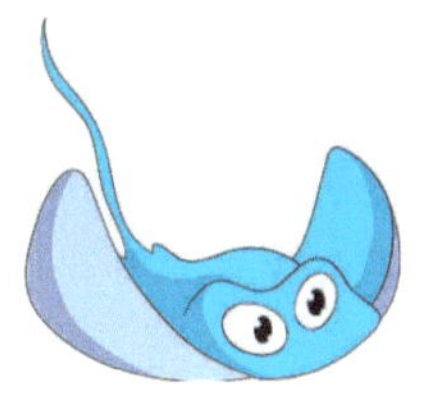

The **manta ray** is an extremely interesting animal. Upon first glance, you will notice that not many other animals look like it. The **manta ray** has a broad head and triangular fins. The larger species of **manta rays** is about 23 feet in width while the smaller species of manta rays is about 18 feet in width.

The average grown-up is a little less than 6 feet tall, so you can imagine how wide this animal is. The **manta ray** also has two *horn-shaped fins* that are located on the front of their heads. Because **manta rays** have these horns, one of its nicknames is the *"devil fish"*.

Manta rays are found in many of our planet's oceans. Most often, they stick around very *warm waters*. Not only is it easier for **manta rays** to live in warmer water, but they often find it easier to find food there. While they may travel into colder waters, they make warmer waters their home.

Another key characteristic of the **manta ray** is that it *travels* a lot every day. In fact, the **manta ray** travels around *43 miles* per day. **This is a huge number**. You and your friends may not even walk one mile per day. **Manta rays** are doing 43 miles today and then they are waking up tomorrow and doing the same thing.

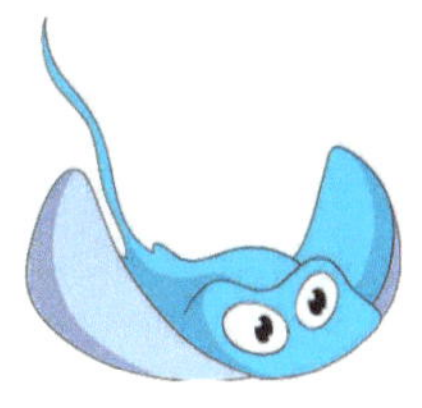

One key reason why the **manta ray** travels so far every day is that it needs to swim *constantly* to stay alive. Unlike us, **manta rays** can't just stay in one place and breathe. **Manta rays** must constantly be on the move in order to get enough oxygen to survive. So the next time you go to an aquarium and see a **manta ray**, don't be surprised to see if constantly moving around. It has to do that to survive.

The **manta ray** is also unique among other *sea creatures* due to the *size* of its *brain*. It has the *largest brain* out of all fish. Because of this, **manta rays** are very *intelligent*. Their brains aren't just useful for helping them smartly go about their days. Their brains actually keep them warm. As **manta rays** dive into colder waters, a substance in their brains prevents them from being chilled. This is a key advantage for these animals, as they may sometimes dive deep to find food or escape predators.

At this point, you may be wondering: *what do **manta rays** eat?* I am glad that you asked! Because of their large size, you may think that **manta rays** go hunting in order to eat large fish. In fact, **manta rays** mostly eat *plankton*, *small fish*, and *krill*. They mostly eat *plankton* and *krill* when they are in shallow water. But when they dive to deeper levels (as I mentioned), **manta rays** will try to find small fish. When the **manta ray** is hunting, it slowly swims around its prey.

All of the *plankton* or small fish that it targets naturally form a tight ball, and from there, the **manta ray** quickly swims through the bunched up organisms with its mouth open. This is a creative way to feed and the **manta ray** does it on a regular basis.

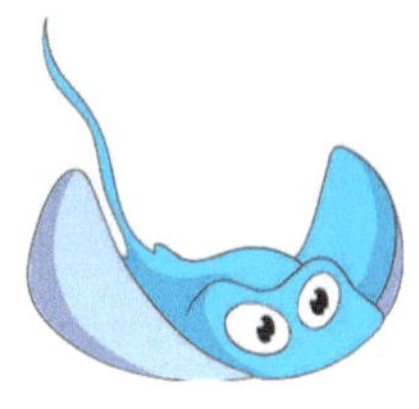

Manta rays don't just look for small fish to eat. In fact, small fish are all too happy to eat parasites on the surface of the *manta ray's body*. It is a quick and easy way for **manta rays** to clean themselves. Pretty cool, right?

When talking about feeding, we also have to discuss who feeds on the **manta ray**. After all, the **manta ray** is part of the food chain. This means that the **manta ray** feeds on **small fish,** but that bigger fish feed on the **manta ray**. For the most part, *large sharks* and *killer whales* are the enemies of **manta rays**. These animals won't hesitate to hunt for **manta rays** in their day-to-day lives. Because of this, **manta rays** must always be on the lookout for these dangerous animals. If they make one mistake, they can be eaten.

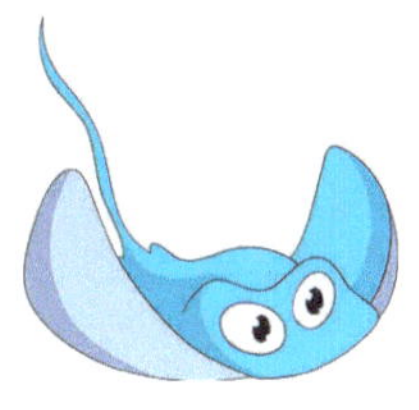

If a **manta ray** is swimming and living in the wild, it can survive for up to *50 years*. This is quite a long time for any type of fish. If the **manta ray** is in an aquarium, it may even be able to survive for longer

Some More Fun Facts

As you can tell by now, manta rays are some of the coolest animals in our oceans. But that's not all. Here are some more fun facts about manta rays. Use these fun facts to impress your friends and family!

The largest manta rays can weigh almost 3,000 pounds.

____

While manta rays often have a white or pale color, but all-black manta rays have been seen in the wild.

____

Manta rays may sometimes leap partially or entirely out of the water.

____

Manta rays have been seen as far from the Equator as North Carolina and New Zealand.

____

Ancient people from Peru used to worship the manta ray.

____

When swimming over deep water, manta rays swim in a straight line. But when they are closer to land, manta rays swim all over the place.

____

Because of their size, few manta rays are found in aquariums.

____

One of the greatest threats to manta rays is overfishing. Fishermen typically catch manta rays with nets or harpoons. Manta rays are primarily fished for their meat, but their bodies can be used for other products.

____

Manta Ray Activities

Counting

Circle the correct answer

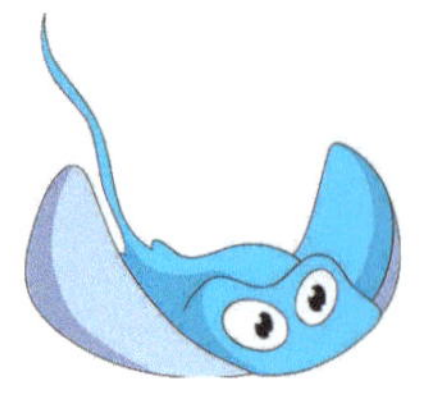

2	1	3
3	2	4
5	4	3
4	5	6

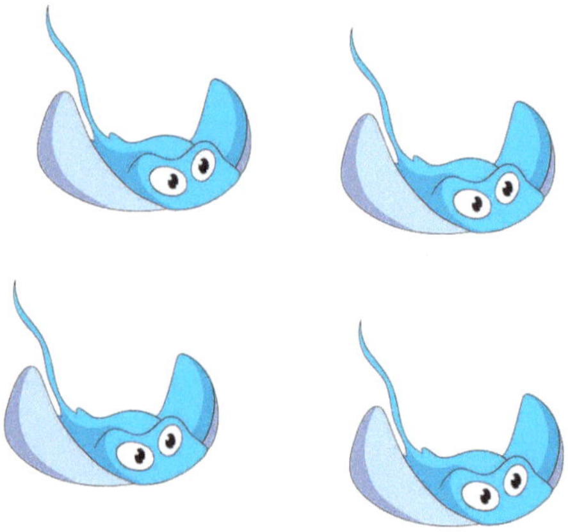

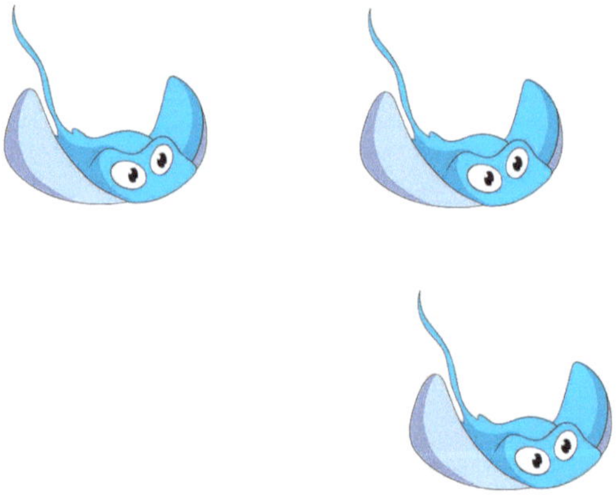

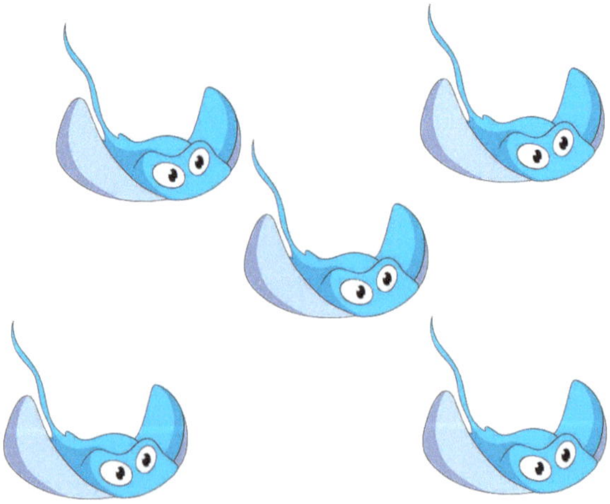

Connect the dots

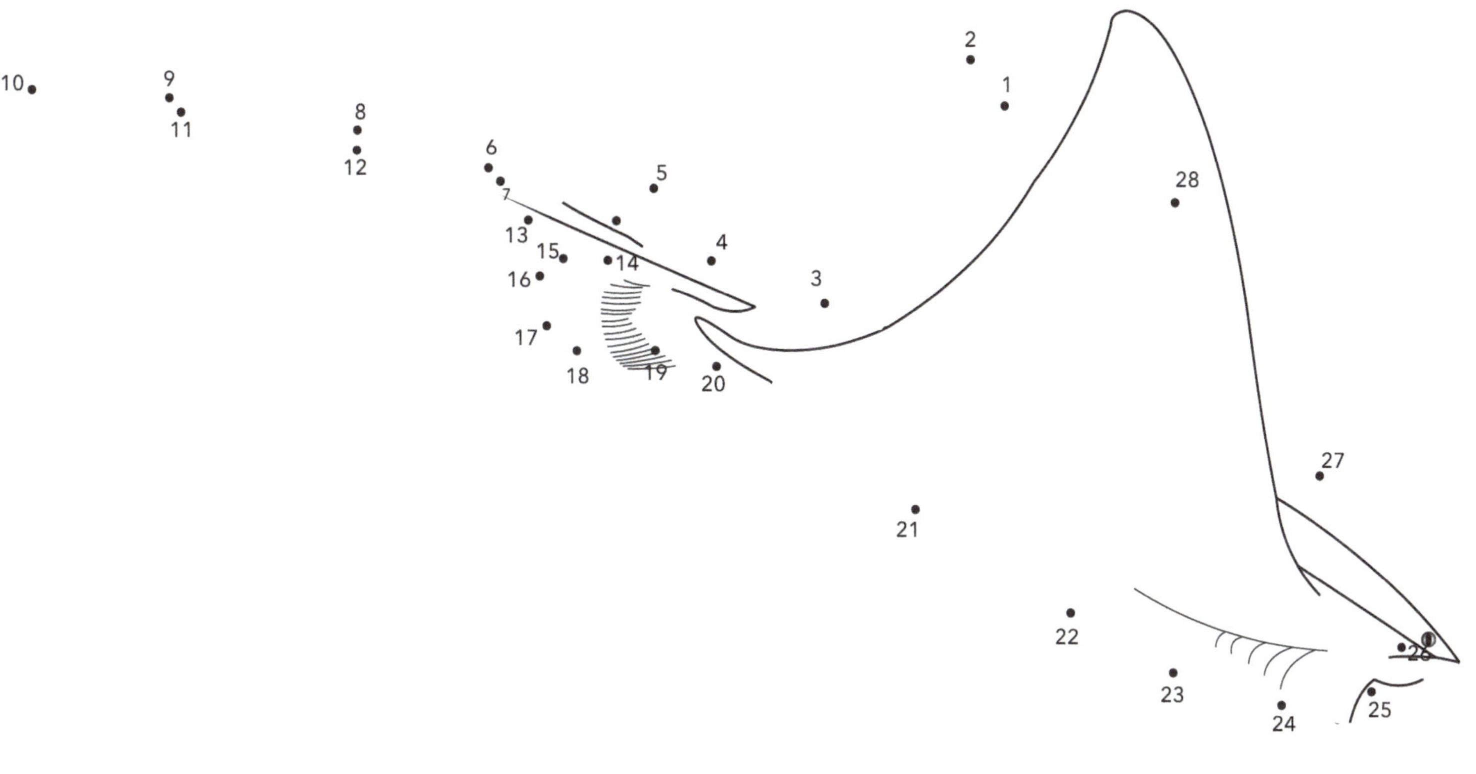

Coloring

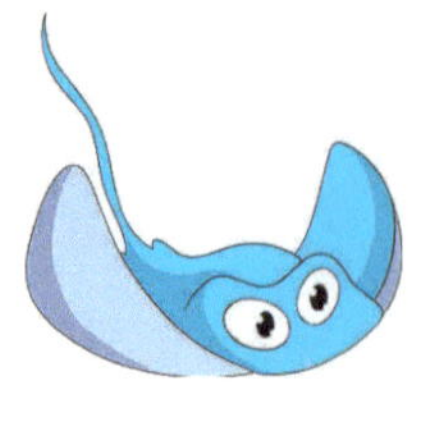

Video & **Quiz** are in our website:

www.adventuresofscubajack.com

Under «**Read To Me**» section